Creating

Service

Superstars

A manager's guide to building your team's
confidence, initiative and commitment to
creating a memorable customer experience

*If you take care of your employees, they
will take care of your customers*

Richard Branson

Caroline Cooper

Published in the United Kingdom by: Naturally Loyal Publications

Book design and layout by Velin@Perseus-Design.com

ISBN: 978-0-9956183-2-9

Disclaimer
All the information, techniques, skills and concepts contained within this publication are of the nature of general comment only, and are not in any way recommended as individual advice.

Should any reader choose to make use of the information contained herein, this is their decision, and the author and publisher does not assume any responsibilities whatsoever under any conditions or circumstances.

Contents

Foreword

Of all the people in a business who can make a difference to the customer experience – the Customer Service Team Members are certainly ideally placed.

Yes – sales people bring in the customers then customer service – keeps them!

Caroline Cooper's new book is a treasure trove of ideas for any customer service team member – and any manager or leader involved in this critical area of the business. In fact – it should be mandatory reading for <u>anyone who touches a customer</u> – regardless of their job title or function.

Caroline's ideas are clearly explained in a simple and logical sequence – each building on the one before. The questions at the end of each chapter ensure the learning points have been recognised and understood. The clever exercises such as Skill/ Will and F.I.R.M. will delight any manager/leader.

This book is a self-learning tool anyone interested in improving service will benefit from as they apply the ideas, methods and systems.

If you have customers and want to delight them, surprise them and keep them – then Caroline Cooper's 'Creating Service Superstars' – is the book you've been waiting for – that's for certain!

Peter Thomson

"The UK's Leading Strategist on Business and Personal Growth"

Introduction

> "I've learned that people will forget what you said, people will forget what you did, but people will never forget how you made them feel."
>
> Maya Angelou

Service v Experience

We know it makes us feel good when we get outstanding customer service. It invariably tempts us to spend more; it encourages us to come back a second or third time and it makes us more confident to refer that business to our family, friends or colleagues.

But the service alone isn't enough. It's how it leaves us feeling which is the difference. Someone can make all the right moves, but without the empathy, rapport or enthusiasm behind it, the service can still leave us feeling cold.

It's the **experience** you create for customers that gets remembered.

Get this right and your customers will not only remember you, they'll spend more, come back more often and recommend you to others.

Which means you need to spend less money, time and effort on your marketing.

It means less worry about where your next new customers are going to come from.

And ultimately it means **more profit**.

The service your customers receive and how this leaves them **feeling** is your single biggest marketing opportunity. It becomes part of your brand and the number one way to **differentiate** your business from your competition.

Don't leave it to chance.

Customer Perception

Of course so much of the customer's experience is based on their own perceptions.

The **emotions** you create for your customers will certainly influence these perceptions. And the emotions of your team will undoubtedly impact those of your customers.

Bored, disengaged, apathetic staff can do serious damage to how your customers perceive their experience. And it only takes one or two team members to 'infect' the entire team.

But when your team are happy this inevitably rubs off on your customers too.

And when your customers are happy they're a lot easier to deal with, which makes life easier for you and your team. So you have a happier team (and fewer staffing headaches!).

So it's a positive virtuous cycle.

More than a tick box training exercise

I hope by now you'll recognise developing a true service culture is more than just a sheep dip customer service training exercise for your front line team.

Getting your team involved, engaged and committed to customer service requires not only a skilled team, but the right infrastructure, support and resources.

This includes support from non-customer facing teams too. Service is everyone's responsibility and anyone in your team can ultimately impact the customers' experience.

With the best will in the world if you don't have these in place even the most skilled and enthusiastic team members will struggle to keep positive about delivering great service.

If you know the experience your customers receive can impact their perception of value when they buy from you, and you depend on your team to deliver that customer experience, let's ensure it's always a good one.

Terminology

To keep things simple throughout the book I refer to customers, which could relate to guests, visitors, delegates, patients, members, clients, etc; whatever is relevant to your business.

I've used the term *team* rather than *staff* or *employees*, so it can encompass suppliers, joint-venture partners, colleagues, support functions, associates; in essence anyone who represents your business and can ultimately impact your customers' experience in any way.

Chapter 4 focuses on developing your team. In many cases I talk of *training*; this might include informal demonstration, on the job coaching, buddying as well as more formal group training.

Getting the most from the book

At the end of each chapter there are some suggested actions. Completing these as you go will help you apply the principles discussed before moving on to the next chapter.

If you prefer to print out the questions and write out your responses you'll find templates for the questions at www.creatingservicesuperstars.com

Before we get started ...

In chapter 2 we'll be discussing the importance of defining your expectations and what great looks like. So with this in mind set your expectations for reading this book!

By knowing what you want to get out of the book you'll know what you are looking for as you read each chapter. You can then apply it to your specific objectives.

I'm sure you'll agree that makes sense.

So do it now...

Actions

- What's your overall aim for reading this book? What do you envisage you will be doing, or be able to do as a result of finishing the book?

- How will this help you, or the business as a whole?

- What are the areas you find most challenging in engaging your team?

- Who can you use as a mentor or sounding board to help talk through your ideas and keep the momentum going?

- Thinking about these challenges what is the biggest benefit for you if you could resolve these?

- On a scale of 1-10 (with 1 being not at all and 10 being critical) how important is this to you?

- If you've answered < 7 what else would you need to get from this book to raise its level of importance?

1

Why Bother

The starting point of all achievement is desire.

Napoleon Hill

When you get home from work can you normally sense what sort of mood everyone at home is in? Even when no words are spoken it's usually pretty easy to tell. Likewise, our own moods and emotions are usually evident to others from our behaviours, body language, facial expressions and tone.

Of course it's no different for customers. They soon pick up when team members are bored, hesitant, impatient or simply disinterested.

And this doesn't just apply to the person they're dealing with directly; the behaviours of anyone else in sight or within earshot can impact how the customer feels.

Irrespective of whether you're selling products or services, in person, by phone or online, the emotions you create in your customer will always have a part to play on their buying decision: their willingness to buy at all, how quickly they buy, how much they spend, their perception of value, their readiness to buy again and their confidence to recommend you.

But sometimes your team don't recognise just how big an impact they can have, or why it is important.

Get Committed

Before we talk about your team let's consider what importance you place on service and the customer experience.

What does customer service mean to you? Why is it important to your business?

Exercise

Define what a great customer experience means to you and your business:

- Take a sheet of A4 paper. Draw a line down the middle. On the left hand side head up the column "What does delivering a memorable customer experience mean to my business?"

- List as many reasons as you can think of.

- Now in the right hand column go back to each reason and ask yourself "What does this mean to me?"

- Now pick your **top 5 compelling reasons** for devoting time to invest in managing your customer experience.

OK, so now <u>you're</u> 100% bought in, but what about your team? You recognise there's room for improvement, but you need their commitment too.

In my experience there are three common objections to any form of change to the way they serve customers:

- But, that's what we do already...

- Well, we've always done it this way...

- I can't...

But, that's what we do already...

As far as your team are concerned they think they are doing a really good job already, so any discussion on customer service standards or suggestion to make changes is seen as a criticism.

This is a common response when your expectation is to improve the standard. They may well be doing an OK job already, but you know it could be better.

I was starkly reminded of this recently when I was asked to deliver some training for the customer facing team of a property services business. The customer feedback clearly indicated there were several areas where improvements were needed to the customer experience, and these were discussed and agreed with my client.

Unfortunately when I started to speak to the team they were blissfully unaware of any of this feedback and so naturally felt they were already doing a great job. It was unsurprising then when they were resistant to any suggestion of change.

So when your team believe they are already doing a good job, start by recognising the things they're already doing well. But be clear about what great looks like (we'll cover this more in the next chapter), and where the gaps are.

In the case above sharing the customer feedback would have been a useful starting point to help them understand the gaps. And even if they didn't agree with the customers' comments, what they could not argue with were the customers' perceptions. Which means the focus would be on what led to those perceptions, and how to change them.

You'll need to take a sensitive approach, and help the team understand how subtle changes can make a difference to the customer's perspective.

Well we've always done it this way...

Why are some people so stuck in the past and their old ways of doing things?

There's a multitude of reasons why some are reluctant to attempt to do anything differently, even though they may recognise it's inevitable or for the better. It's not an unusual response to shy away from change. Whilst some might rise to the challenge you're just as likely to have people who'll resist anything that takes them away from their old comfortable way of doing things.

One of the first ways to overcome this is to explain the reason **why**. Why do things any differently. This isn't just stating why it's important from a company perspective, but focusing on WIIFM.

i.e. What's In It For Me; from the **team's perspective** rather than yours.

Put yourself in their shoes... Will it make my job easier? Will it free up time to focus on other things that are important to me? Will it mean I get fewer complaints? Will it mean I can earn more tips? Will it make my job more enjoyable? Will it give me more pride in what I do? Will it make me more confident? Will it mean I get more recognition?

We often think the benefits are obvious. However the team will generally home in on the downsides first. More work. Something new to learn. It's too complicated. I'm too old to change. It won't work. We tried it before.

Of course there are business benefits too, and we don't need to shy away from these, but sometimes they think of these as being only in the owner's or management's favour. What they often don't see is the impact a healthy business can have on them: More opportunities, greater investment in the business, better equipment, improved conditions, more job security.

What are the knock-on effects of the business doing well? The local community, your suppliers, employment prospects, building your reputation, and so on.

I can't...

Even when you've sold them on the idea of doing things differently to create a better customer experience you still can't guarantee they'll embrace the change.

Look out for and listen for hesitation. When you hear comments such as *"I can't do that"* find out what's prompted that reaction. Is there still a lack of willingness because they're not yet convinced it's worth the extra effort? Or is it a matter of skill or capability?

"I can't..." might simply mean a lack of confidence, and they're in need of some reassurance, coaching or practice. Perhaps there are other skills that are a prerequisite, which they don't yet have. Or, worse they fear it will expose other weaknesses they feel they have.

"I can't…" could mean they haven't got all the resources they need. Maybe there's special equipment needed, or a budget they don't have. Perhaps they don't think they have the time, or know what they can leave out instead to make time.

"I can't…" may be because they've simply not been allowed to do this before. Old systems, processes or procedures have prevented them, and despite the fact you've moved on nobody as yet has set out the new 'rules', or demonstrated their faith in them to do it.

So irritating as it might be when your team turn around and say "but, we've always done it this way" don't give up in frustration! Give them a **compelling** enough reason and the support they need to do it the 'new' way.

And of course old habits die hard, so continue to encourage, support and guide them whilst they **embed their new habits.**

Actions

- List or create a mind map of all the potential benefits and spin offs for your team in delivering an improved customer experience.

- Knowing your team, what are the potential objections they might raise to doing things any differently?

- How might you respond to these objections?

2

What Great Looks Like

In order to carry a positive action we must develop here a positive vision.

Dalai Lama

Before we can hope to manage our customer experience we need to define what that experience is.

When I start working with a business I often find they don't have any clearly defined ideas of what good service looks like; they just know they'll recognise it when they see it.

This isn't particularly helpful when you're trying to convey to others what you expect!

Lack of clarity leads to confusion for your team, inconsistencies for your customers and frustration for you.

What does great customer service look like, sound like or feel like for you?

Do your team know what great (or even good or acceptable) looks like? How will they know when they are doing things right? Do they know what they're aiming for?

Although you may not want to be totally prescriptive, you'll at least want to define minimum expectations, as everyone's interpretation and perspective can differ. The better they understand your end goal the easier it will be for them to deliver the customer experience you are aiming for.

It's not just about the behaviours you expect your team to demonstrate in dealing with customers, but defining the whole of the customer experience from end to end.

If everyone understands what you're looking to achieve it makes it so much easier to make decisions based on this outcome. It becomes a part of your culture and way of doing things. And it certainly makes training easier as you know exactly what you're aiming for.

Values

Your values are your way of saying "this is what's important to us". They represent a way to share beliefs that define your culture.

When we talk about **customer service values** it's a way of describing what we see as important in how we treat our customers. Naturally your customer service values must tie in with the whole ethos, culture and brand identity of the business.

The clearer your values the easier it is going to be to define how you will deliver them and communicate these to everyone else involved.

If you don't already have your service criteria clearly defined start by defining your company values and expectations towards the customer experience. What is the style and ethos of your business, and how is this reflected in the way you serve your customers?

What do your customers value most?

Naturally there needs to be a correlation between what's important to you and what's important to your customers.

This has to start with an understanding of who your ideal customers are and what's important for them, what your customers expect and how **they** define great service.

When everyone in your business has the same snapshot of the ideal customer it's so much easier to define the ideal customer experience you're working on. This in turn means it's easier for every effort to add value.

Ask yourself not just **who** they are, but identify what need you're meeting or **problem you are solving.**

Why do your customers buy from **you** specifically? What makes **your** business, venue, offer or service different? Why is **your** experience better than anyone or anywhere else?

Recognising your customers' highest **priorities** and level of **importance** means you can make sure you deliver these above all else.

What's the experience you're trying to create?

There's a difference between what people need and what they want. You only have to think of what happens when you go shopping. How often have you come home from a shopping trip with far more than you intended to buy?

Over 50% of the customer's experience is down to **emotions**. So we have to go beyond just what our customers need. Identify what they really care about, and define the emotions you want to create for your customers.

Here are two examples:

Example 1

*Imagine your business is a **visitor attraction**: Your typical holiday season visitor **needs** to keep their children entertained. But what they **care about** is their children are being educated, and that they are getting plenty of exercise and fresh air..... They want to **feel** energised, have fun and relaxed that their children are safe.*

Example 2

*If you are a **letting agent**: The landlord **needs** his property let and to know his rent is being collected, but what he **cares about** is that his property is being cared for and monitored. So he **wants to feel** trust, reassurance and peace of mind.*

*On the other hand as a letting agent your tenants **need** somewhere in the right location at the right price. What they want from the property will vary from tenant to tenant. But they will inevitably **care about** comfort and value for money, so they want to **feel** trust in their agent and reassurance that any issues will be dealt with swiftly.*

So we've considered the difference between the physical and rational needs of your customer and the emotional aspects and how they want to be feeling. By recognising these less tangible aspects you have a way to **differentiate yourself from your competitors** who on the face of it could be offering exactly the same products or services.

What feelings or emotions do you or could you create for your customers which means a customer buys **from you** opposed to others who could also meet their (rational or physical) need?

These will become what you're remembered for.

Piecing it together

Once everyone in your business understands your ideal customer and what's important to them it's going to be so much easier to deliver this point of **differentiation**.

Taking into account your customer service values, ideal customers and what's important to them, and the emotions we want to create you're now in a position to start defining what great service and a great customer experience should look like and feel like.

It's easy to assume that this should be obvious, but when it comes to customer service phrases such as 'being polite' or 'giving a warm welcome' these can be interpreted differently by different people.

Your culture and values should be evident in EVERYTHING you do. Define how these values will be evident in the **ideal customer experience**.

If you can't describe or demonstrate what good looks like how will your team know when they're doing it right?

It's so important you can define exactly what behaviours (i.e. what you expect to hear people say or see them do) constitute your customer service standards.

In other words what does great look like?

The more tangible they are the easier it becomes for your team to monitor their own performance and know how they are doing at any one moment in time.

Actions

- How would you define your customer service values?

- What does giving a great experience mean to you?

- What is the style and ethos of your business?

- What do you want to be remembered for?

- Who are your customers?

- What aspects of service do your customers value most?

- How would you define the type of experience you're trying to create?

- What feelings or emotions do you want to create for your customers?

- What behaviours would you expect to see to achieve this?

- Identify examples of where your team members are already demonstrating each of the values.

Once you've completed it for yourself, ask your management team to answer each of the questions.

Finally ask your whole team to answer the questions (not just customer facing).

It will be interesting to see if you all agree!

3

Walk a Mile in their Shoes

"...Just walk a mile in his moccasins
Before you abuse, criticize and accuse.
If just for one hour, you could find a way
To see through his eyes, instead of your
own muse..."

From the poem *Judge Softly* by Mary T. Lathrap

If you've never experienced your business from a customer's perspective you can only guess at what it's like to be a customer.

How often do any of your team (or you for that matter!) put yourself in your customers' shoes?

When did they last see, hear and feel everything your customers might experience?

I'm saddened when I meet team members who only know their tiny little bit of the customer journey, and don't have a clue what else the customer gets to see, hear or feel.

I strongly encourage you to have **every single team member** experience **every one of your customer touch points**. It isn't just the responsibility of the reception or customer service desk; everyone contributes in some way to the customer experience either directly or indirectly. So **involve everyone**.

This has two spin offs.

Firstly you get a fresh pair of eyes (and ears) on what the customer sees, hears or experiences.

Of course this is no substitute for your customers' feedback, but it's amazing what team members will spot as opportunities to enhance or modify what happens at a touch point to give a smoother or enhanced customer experience. Not forgetting the potential it opens up for them subsequently spotting opportunities to add value or make recommendations to customers.

Secondly it helps your team members to engage more readily with your customers.

Because they've experienced the customer journey first hand they are able to appreciate what's important to the customer at that point, and can more readily relate to them when discussing or describing any aspect of your service or products.

Of course it may not always be possible for team members to experience everything (let's say you are a midwife or undertaker!). But even if you sell exotic holidays or exclusive wedding dresses there will still be plenty of opportunity to get a sense of what your customers experience, particularly the various touch points your customer experiences before or after doing business with you, which so often gets forgotten.

If your team find it difficult to relate to what a customer might expect (such as luxury services or products your team members may not have experienced for themselves first-hand) relate back to the emotions you are looking to evoke as discussed in the last chapter. The better they really understand the outcome you're aiming for the easier it will be for them to work out how to deliver it.

Because we can become oblivious to what we're involved in every day (and sometimes be quite protective), aim to mix up your departments, so they are not just looking at their own work area. Even old hands can give you another perspective by experiencing another department.

Build it into your induction process as new team members will be experiencing things for the first time, giving you a fresh perspective (as well as providing them with a great introduction to your business).

Map the entire journey

When reviewing your customer journey ensure it covers all the touch points. A customer's experience starts way before they actually set foot in your business (even if entering it in the virtual sense).

It takes into account how they first hear about you, what they hear about you or read about you, their experience when they Google you and when they first make contact.

It also identifies what happens once they've concluded their business with you; what follow-up they get, their lasting memories of you, the response they receive if they have a follow-up enquiry or question.

For a customer journey map to be really effective, it must also include the irrational sides of the experience i.e. the emotions created and subconscious messages.

This includes identifying how your customers might be feeling entering the experience.

For example:

If your business is a firm of solicitors...

*Customers coming to you for conveyancing for buying their first home might well be entering the experience with a sense of **anticipation, excitement,** and a degree of **nervousness** about the commitment they're making.*

*Whereas, if they're seeking legal advice - maybe due to a business dispute or a divorce - they'll be experiencing very different emotions at the start of the customer journey; maybe **anger, frustration** or **upset**.*

Once your team fully understand how your customers might be feeling at that very first point of contact it makes it far easier for them to build rapport and have empathy with your customers right from the outset.

How well do your team understand the typical life cycle for a customer? For example: How long a lead-in time is there likely to be before they buy from you? Will customers be shopping around and making comparisons before making a decision? Do they need to establish trust in you before they buy from you? How well informed will they be from previous experience or online research?

Understanding the steps the customer will take helps appreciate the customer's perspective and how they can influence the customer's first impression.

If there are different routes to purchase list them all out separately, focusing on one route at a time. Or better still create a flow diagram or decision tree so you can map out each individual touch point of the customer's journey.

Don't fall down at the final fence

Imagine you're celebrating a special occasion with friends. You've had a fantastic evening. You've been well cared for, attended to with fantastic hospitality. Your meal was wonderful, the atmosphere was relaxed and all your friends and family have had a good time.

But when it's time to get the bill suddenly no one is interested. Nobody wants to take your money! You pay a visit to the toilets and they are a mess. You overhear staff complaining about a customer. When your waiter finally takes your payment it's rushed and curt.

If this has ever happened to you you'll know how much this influences your biding memory.

One of the most important determining factors in prompting a positive lasting memory and potential repeat purchase is what happens in the very last few minutes of a customer's experience.

Your customer journey map should also identify the touch points following their 'purchase'. (I use the term purchase in a generic sense. For example if you're a chiropractor your customers probably don't think of it as a purchase as such, so substitute the word purchase with treatment, appointment, or whatever best suits your business.)

What's the very last touch point at the point of purchase; for example a confirmation or thank you message, a farewell, a follow-up invitation, invitation for feedback, etc.

If you are a bricks and mortar business what's the **very last thing** your customers see, hear, smell, taste or feel as they leave?

What's going on behind the scenes you'd rather your customers didn't see? The last conversation they hear as they leave, the state of the back office, over flowing bins, your team having a cigarette by the back door, a disgruntled security guard or off duty team members fooling around?

Unless your team get to experience all of these things for themselves they will never fully understand just how important they are.

If your customers only ever get to speak to you by phone what's the last thing they hear?

How well do your team understand the need for customers to feel appreciated? And how easy it is for them to unintentionally make signs that they've other more important things to be getting on with?

How sensitive is your team at picking up when the customer is in a hurry and they need to speed up.

If you're an online business what happens at the end of the transaction that reassures your customer everything's gone through smoothly.

Even if everything your customer experiences up to this point has been seamless and perfect it's those last few moments which influence the end result - how they feel, what they say, and what they do as a result of doing business with you. So don't let it all fall down at the final fence.

But it's not down to **us** ...

One of the 'excuses' I often hear is that it's down to a third party provider and they have no control over it. Think about this. These suppliers could be your customers' very first impression (such as the security guard at your site, the reception desk at your serviced offices or call answering service) or very last impression (e.g. as in your delivery or courier firm).

The two most critical touch points of your customers' journey - and you're leaving it to chance with your suppliers?

It's just as important if not more so to get these right too.

Moments of truth

Ask your team to map out their understanding of your customer journey listing all the possible touch points, then pin point the key points which are likely to have the most impact on your customers. For example as we've identified the very first impression and the very last touch point are both critical in most businesses. What other points on the customer journey will be most influential?

Once they've identified these it's important to understand the experience you want to create for the customer at each part of the customer journey.

We've already discussed how **emotions** matter. They are a key driver for the customer. If your team can imagine the emotions you want your customers to feel **at each of these critical stages** of the customer journey then they'll be in a far better place to meet these.

When customers first call you how do you want them to feel? Intrigued? Inspired? Informed? Relieved? What experience do you want them to have? Easy? Quick? Informative? Excited? Or would feeling reassured, confident and calm be more appropriate for your customers?

What's the very last impression you want to leave with a customer? Do you want to leave a Wow factor or a positive biding memory? Or is feeling informed, trusting, or confident more important?

The better your team understand your customers and what's important at each stage the easier this will be.

Here are a couple of examples to demonstrate this.

Example 1

Imagine your business is a restaurant

*When customers first hear about you, you might want to create some **interest** or **curiosity**, possibly some **excitement** about dining with you.*

*Leading up to the date of the booking but before customers arrive you might want to ensure they feel **confident** and **relaxed** about finding you, but also a sense of **anticipation**, looking forward to the occasion.*

*At the point they enter the restaurant you want them to feel **welcomed, relaxed** and **comfortable**. When they leave you want them to feel **appreciated, cared for, happy** and **relaxed**.*

Example 2

If you run an IT support company

*Bearing in mind when a customer makes contact with you it may be due to a problem they need sorted quickly. So they might already be feeling frustration or even anger. So when they first make contact the desired emotion is one of **reassurance, trust, confidence, calm**.*

*If their issue can't be sorted instantly you want them to feel **important, informed, reassured**.*

*Once you fix their issue if it's something which could have been avoided you'll want customers to feel **confident, knowledgeable, reassured** (or to avoid the problem happening again), **trust** in you, **valued**.*

Can you see how thinking through the **emotions** you want to create at each of the **key touch points** helps your team start to think about what they need to do at each point to ensure they give customers the best experience?

If they understand the emotions you want to create for customers they are much more likely to achieve the end result.

Reality Check

Now it's time for the reality check; how well do you achieve this currently?

Ask your team to make an honest assessment and reflect on how they think **customers** currently feel at each of these key touch points.

If they aren't sure ask them to reflect back on some of the conversations they've had with customers.

Next arrange for each team member to take the customer journey themselves and see how it feels being on the receiving end.

If you've done this exercise with your team before this time allocate team members to different departments to get a different perspective. When it's your own department it's easy to become protective, oblivious to some of the challenges or frustrations customers may encounter. Reviewing another department can help flush out potential 'blind spots'.

As they work through/experience the customer journey for themselves ask them to note down how it leaves them feeling at each of the touch points. If your desired emotion is confidence, trust, clarity, are you achieving this or do they feel confused, sceptical, frustrated.

If the reality doesn't match up to the emotions you want customers to feel ask them to identify **why not**. What did they spot that is not working quite as it should be?

For example: is it down to how messages are presented, is it down to branding, is there too much red tape, is it something a colleague does or says, is it response times...?

Ask your team to make a note of everything that isn't quite perfect yet. It doesn't mean to say you have to fix everything, but you can make a conscious decision as to which aspects you might put to one side for now and which need to be addressed as a priority.

It can be quite revealing what your team pick up; they'll often spot things you don't.

This is a great way to flush out anything that's standing in the way of them doing a great job and will often highlight frustrations they have in the system or with current resources, levels of authority, existing skills or conflicting priorities.

Listen to what they have to say

Listen to what your team tell you about shortfalls in the customer journey; they'll invariably spot where improvements can be made.

Unless followed though promptly, any potential barriers will simply provide an excuse for them not to deliver the service standards you expect.

The longer problems are left unresolved, the less emphasis it places on customer service in their eyes and the less importance they will place on their contribution to delivering a great experience.

Actions

- Ask your team to identify the critical customer touch points. (This is easiest done on post it notes initially so you can move them around or add touch points as they identify them.)

- Next define the emotion(s) you want to create at each of these touch points

- Ask each team member to complete the customer journey (or a section) and note specifically how it feels at each key touch point

- What are their observations?

- What's good?

- Where are there potential shortfalls?

- What needs tweaking?

- What are your priority actions?

4

Tricks of the Trade

If you can't explain it simply, you don't understand it well enough.

Albert Einstein

Relying on employees to pick things up as they go along can lead to picking up bad habits, mixed messages and ultimately poor performance and wasted resources.

But depending on experienced team members to pass on their skills to others does not always work; just because they are good at doing something doesn't necessarily mean they're willing or able to explain it to others.

So having a planned approach to training, coaching and supporting your team in customer service skills is a fundamental part of building your team's confidence and willingness to deliver great service.

Skill Will

In simplistic terms there are 2 factors that will influence somebody's performance in any task. These are:

- Skill: their level of skill, capability and knowledge

- Will: their willingness, motivation and enthusiasm

	Low Will	High Will
High Skill	'The problem child'	'The Star Performer'
Low Skill	'The under-achiever'	'The Apprentice'

The two go hand-in-hand for creating 'star performers'. So in this chapter we'll focus on the skill aspect and in the next chapter we'll focus on the will.

We could add a 3rd dimension to this model which is the provision of the right resources, tools and time and we'll be covering this aspect in chapter 6.

What training?

Obviously what skills and knowledge training you give your team will be in line with your customer service standards, their current capabilities and the specific requirements of their role.

Consider the scope of your training and what other knowledge may help up front. Then structure your training accordingly.

The scope of this book does not allow us to go into detail on training content, but here are some considerations when planning training for your team. As well as helping you plan your content, you can be thinking about the best way to deliver this to develop your team and gain their buy-in.

Skills

Your team needs to understand the mechanics of caring for customers. How to establish rapport; how to ask open questions to identify what the customer wants; how to listen actively to customers' requests or preferences; how to respond, make suggestions, or offer alternatives that best meet the customers' needs.

Give them **examples** of how they would welcome customers, how they might describe each of your products and services, or handle difficult questions.

But, **instead of a script**, allow them to develop their own dialogue, one that comes naturally to them, rather than something they have to remember and run the risk of forgetting.

Sometimes you may need to put the subject matter into context.

For example: dealing with customer complaints. You could simply cover the procedures for dealing with a complaint. But knowing how to understand customers, how to ask questions and build rapport are pre requisites to dealing with complaints effectively.

Knowledge

Customers want and expect your team to be able to give accurate information on your products and service so they can make an informed choice.

In order to sell, upsell, or cross sell, as a minimum your team need to understand all the offers, products and services you provide. This goes beyond just a laundry list; it needs to include understanding of the features and of course the benefits from a **customer's perspective**.

What's included in a package, what are the different options, what are their recommendations or suggested combinations? A good understanding of your customers' profile, needs and expectations will help this process.

When I'm working with some businesses I'm often somewhat alarmed by the lack of exposure staff have to other departments.

As examples: On a support desk - do your team actively use any of the products on which they're providing support? In a hotel - have any of your reservations team ever set foot in the spa, or seen first-hand the difference between a standard and an executive room? At a leisure centre - have any of your receptionists ever experienced a class? In a travel business - have any of the consultants ever flown with the airline in question or seen the resort they are recommending (even if only a virtual view)? In a law firm - do the support teams understand what documents or actions need completing before they can start discussions on conveyancing? In a restaurant - have all the team tasted every dish on the menu?

Your team can never hope to convey to customers all the benefits of these products or services if they'd never had any first-hand experience, let alone describe them with any enthusiasm or feeling, or have empathy with customers when they're trying to resolve problems.

You won't necessarily be able to cover every conceivable angle. Such as, as a law firm you wouldn't expect your receptionists to have experienced the services of a defence lawyer! But they still need to understand what the lawyers do and who to refer customers to dependent on the query.

Spot the opportunities

The more of your products and services your team experience for themselves the more confident they'll be to talk about them, and the more willingness there will be for them to promote if and when appropriate.

Help your team identify all the situations that lend themselves as an opportunity to wow your customers or add extra value. This might include pre-empting customer needs, remembering specific preferences or simply making personal recommendations or suggestions to help the customer.

It will certainly be easier to evoke an emotional appeal through vivid descriptions of feel, appearance, taste, smell, if they've been there themselves.

Anticipate (what if...)

Equip your team to deal with the unexpected. In any business there are times when things don't go according to plan or mishaps happen. The more you can anticipate these and train your team in how to handle such situations the more confident they'll be, and the likely they'll deal smoothly with anything that crops up.

If your goal is to minimise the negative impact on the customer experience teach them how to do this! For example: how to minimise the impact of queues, what to do when a customer makes a scene, how to apologise without losing face when they make a mistake on a customer's order or when something the customer really wants is no longer available.

It's easy for the team members to get flustered when it goes wrong, so make this part of your training.

Of course, not every member of your team needs to be expert in everything, but it always helps if they 'know a man who can' so they can refer to or call on the appropriate person when needed to deal with a specific customer situation, request or query.

Levels of authority

There's nothing more frustrating for a customer and demotivating for a team member than saying *"I don't have the authority to do that; I'll need to get my manager."* Of course, this wastes your time too, when you're called over to deal with the situation.

So establish up front what levels of authority your team members have in any given situation. Define these levels of authority when training, and give them examples of when they need to refer to a manager or get sign off, and when it's OK for them to make the decision.

Give your team a sense of ownership and pride by encouraging them to come forward with their own ideas of how the customer experience can be improved and make every effort to take their ideas on board.

What result

When conducting formal training set objectives so you have a clear picture of what people should be taking away from the training.

Think of your outcomes in actionable terms. "To understand the importance of customer service" means nothing. What do you want people **to do** differently as a result of the activity?

What are the behaviours you want to see, what do you want to hear team members saying, what do you want customers to be feeling, saying or doing, and by when?

Why do I need to know this?

Don't waste yours and the team's time in training them in things they don't need. Who wants to sit through training that is either a repeat of what they have already done, insults their intelligence as they are already doing what the training is intended to achieve or is irrelevant to their job?

If there is a shortfall determine if this is a matter of skill or are there other reasons such as a lack of resources, or mixed messages about what's expected or a lack of motivation on their part.

As we discussed in chapter 1, it's easy to assume people who need training already recognise their shortfalls or the need for training. But sadly they're often still blissfully unaware of any need to do anything any differently, unless they've had feedback to highlight the gap.

Trying to teach someone something from this point is a fundamental reason a lot of training fails. Without recognition they will not be receptive to learning and the barriers will go up thinking *"this doesn't apply to me"*.

Once they are conscious of the need to learn they still may not be motivated to do anything about it. Stimulate interest by highlighting its relevance to their role and why it's important.

Will it make their job easier, quicker, safer, or more interesting or fun? Will it give them more confidence and independence in their role?

Occasionally you'll see a reluctance to carry out certain activities as it feels uncomfortable. For example: team members might shy away from *"upselling"*. They don't want to be pushy or be seen to be manipulating customers into buying something they don't want.

A simple change of language can change their perception. In this example instead of referring to *"upselling"* describe it as *"adding value"*.

Make training engaging

The last thing you want when training is to see a sea of glum faces in front of you, and know the minute the team walks away it will be back to business as normal; acting on nothing they've learnt.

Whenever I'm training I live by my **FIRM** principles.

These are to make training:

Fun. Allowing people to have fun while they learn makes them more receptive and engaged (important for you) and enjoyable (important for the team). Smiling and laughter trigger dopamine, which in turn turns on all the learning centres in the brain.

Take people away from their normal environment (as long as this doesn't make them feel uncomfortable or become a distraction). Conduct the training outside, use music, alter the room or room layout, introduce unusual props.

Keep in mind delegates' schedules and personal circumstances. It won't be much fun if team members have already done a full shift or go straight from the training back to work. They'll have little chance of either being receptive to the training or have time to absorb what they've learnt.

Involved. The more people are involved the greater their buy-in to the ideas and principles. You'll also benefit from their insights and ideas which promotes learning from one another, and leads to better teamwork. Avoid chalk and talk (or death by PowerPoint, for that matter).

Use everyday activities as opportunities for development. Use team meetings to direct focus and reinforce messages. Assign tasks or projects on genuine customer service related challenges, identify staff champions, encourage job swaps and cross training for greater flexibility amongst the team.

Ask for their opinions, run exercises, either in groups, or individually, so everyone can share their ideas and benefit from each other's insights and suggestions. Encourage the team to jot down their ideas and share with others as this helps the brain assimilate the information, and starts them thinking about how they will apply their ideas.

Relevant. Theory is fine, but people need to know **how** it can be applied to their own roles. Use relevant examples and illustrations to help people relate to their own job. Otherwise nothing changes, and it's a complete waste of time and money!

Relate your training back to the customer journey. You can use the customer journey review as a pre training activity if you know you won't have time to incorporate it into your training sessions.

Give a specific brief of things to review and bring to any training session. This is a good way to engage the team before it starts.

It's all very well knowing what to do and say, but you know how sometimes when you come to say something the words just don't trip off the tongue as you might hope! Let your team practise in a safe environment, based on different scenarios.

Use role play whilst still in the safety of the training environment so they can practise their new skills to build confidence, and find their own way of saying things in their own voice.

It's all too easy to include everything you possibly can on a topic and overload people with too much or irrelevant information.

They then can't retain it all, become bored and switch off, or you simply run out of time. If you've a clearly identified objective this is your starting point.

If you suspect it's too much to cover in one session it probably is. In which case don't be afraid to break it down into 2 or 3 smaller sessions. It's far better to cover fewer things in depth than to merely skim the surface on a lot of areas, leaving people with insufficient skills or knowledge to really implement any of it effectively.

Memorable. So much training is forgotten in 5 minutes. If you're familiar with the Ebbinghaus effect you'll know the implications of the Ebbinghaus Curve of Forgetting; that your audience forgets most of what you tell them, sometimes within as little as an hour.

You want people to remember the messages, not just tomorrow, but next week, next month and next year!

Avoid thinking about *training* purely as an activity that takes place in a classroom.

Add variety. Do something different to what people are used to, to make it interesting or memorable, so everyone remembers the messages.

Keep messages simple. Use memory aids such as acronyms and diagrams to help everyone remember the key points.

Now what?

The number 1 mistake I see businesses making with their customer service training is not making the transition from theory to the real world.

This starts during the training. Asking for ideas on how team members are going to implement what they have learnt. Help them identify situations where they can put their learning into practice **as quickly as possible,** preferably within the next day or two, and get their commitment to one or two specific actions.

Flush out any questions or concerns, or anything they know of which will make it difficult or even impossible for them to implement what they've learnt. Check they have the necessary resources, time, authority, peer support and opportunity to put it into practice. If not, ensure you get these in place before that momentum is lost.

These might be things you don't want to hear, but better to know about these now (and have an opportunity to put them right) than them going away confused or negative through questions unanswered and discover two weeks on that nothing has changed!

On an individual level this might include a lack of confidence or a concern they might make mistakes. They may be unclear on which actions are their job opposed to anyone else's. They might not even see these actions as part of their role, but somebody else's responsibility.

Be available for individuals to ask questions on a one to one basis after any training; not everyone will feel comfortable raising their queries in front of colleagues, and some may need a while to reflect on what's been covered.

You might want to set some specific medium-term goals to focus people's attention in implementing the training. It might simply be based on customer feedback, or a specific target to sell x number of a certain product or service.

Finish training by giving recognition for their participation. Create a link to further training, or how you'll be following up in the workplace.

Making the transition

Sometimes the only way to really hone new skills and develop true competence is once applied on the job. It simply can't always happen in the confines of the training session or without the pressures of the real world.

We shouldn't expect perfection straight away. People need time to practise and find their own way of doing things, and not be afraid to make the odd mistake so long as they learn from it.

Everything takes longer when it's new and you're still learning a little from trial and error. Confidence can be low as you get to grips with it all.

Unless followed though promptly, any potential barriers will simply provide an excuse for not putting things into practice. The longer problems are left unresolved, the less the likelihood of anyone getting to the point it becomes habit.

So when you plan training, schedule time for team members to practise and time for you or their line manager to check how they are doing. Or assign a mentor, coach or buddy to help overcome the initial barriers to perfecting their new skill.

Observe how team members handle the conversations with customers and give them feedback after the event on what they're doing well, what they could do more of, and give the appropriate coaching, support and guidance on areas where they need more help.

Maintaining Momentum

Provide back up resources such as prompt cards or checklists. Reinforce messages by building exercises into your daily and weekly calendar, etc., as part of team briefings or meetings, 1:1 reviews and ongoing feedback.

Recognise the role line managers have in the follow up to training. What's working well, what fresh perspectives have they brought, what needs more practice?

If the training isn't being implemented identify what's getting in the way now, not wait until they've been struggling and given up hope. When something doesn't work right first time around it's all too easy for them to go back to their old and familiar ways.

It takes time to instil new habits.

Actions

- List all the key skills your team need to deliver your customer service standards.

- List all the information they need to know about your business, products or services.

- What are the potential unexpected situations your team should be confident to deal with as and when they arise?

- Of your existing team where do they sit on the skills/will matrix?

- Who are your star performers who could support, mentor or coach fellow team members?

- Who needs training in what skills and knowledge?
  (There is a matrix in the resource area at
  www.creatingservicesuperstars.com)

- Define what levels of authority your team have.

- What can you incorporate into your training to make it more fun, involved, relevant and memorable?

5

A Sparkling Performance

"Never tell people how to do things.
Tell them what to do and they will surprise
you with their ingenuity."

General S. Patton

Having a happy and productive team is critical to delivering great customer service and a memorable experience. Your team can be your point of differentiation.

So what is the secret to having an engaged, motivated and eager to please team who will add a sparkle to your customers' experience?

We've already looked at the skill axis of the skill / will model…

Now for the will.

Unless your team are **fully engaged** and happy in their job it's unlikely they'll do very much more than deliver mediocre service.

I believe behaviour breeds behaviour.

A miserable team generally leads to a miserable customer experience.

And can often lead to poor performance, poor attendance and ultimately to losing not only your best people, but also losing your valued customers.

But when your team is happy and engaged this rubs off on your customers too.

The basics

Everyone is different; we are all individuals so some things are more important to some than others, but in my experience as a minimum there are five basics which, if we get these right, will go a long way to getting the best from your team.

1. Set your expectations

A lack of direction can be confusing and leads to uncertainty. We've talked a lot already about what great looks like, but of course this needs to be communicated. Not just what is expected of them but how this will be measured, so they can keep track of their own performance and know how they are doing.

Be consistent. Lead by example, so there are no mixed messages. It's easy for different managers to have different expectations and different interpretations of the standards you expect. If these are detailed in behavioural terms and documented it's so much easier for everyone to be consistent. Ensure the same rules apply to everyone and that the rest of your supervisory team are consistent with their expectations.

Focus on telling people what you want to achieve i.e. **the end result**, rather than dictating <u>how</u> to do it. This gives them flexibility to adopt their own style (you'll be surprised how often they end up improving the process) rather than living in fear of not being able to comply with strict processes.

Once you've set your expectations make it possible for your team to reach these by providing the appropriate tools, resources and training to do the job effectively. (We'll talk more about this in chapter 6.)

2. Look and Listen

If you are approachable, when team members do have concerns you get to hear about them before they become a problem. Provide support when needed and be receptive to when it's required; not everyone will be confident enough to ask for help so don't assume that they will just come and ask you when they are unsure.

Listen to and act quickly on staff concerns; left to fester these can snowball into bigger problems, which had they been nipped in the bud would have been easy to resolve.

Consult with team members and listen to their ideas; they may be able to suggest better ways of doing things and will be far more bought in to doing something well if they have initiated it.

Involve the team in decisions by asking for their views. Many of your team are much closer to your customers than you are and will see opportunities to enhance the customer experience. So ask for their ideas and be prepared to act on them.

Clearly if you are someone's line manager they will have an expectation to get guidance from you on how they should do their job. But utilise their potential to develop by putting some of the onus on them to come up with their own suggestions and solutions as often as possible.

Take time to talk to your team to show an interest in them as individuals. This will help build trust (both ways) which will mean your team are far more likely to go the extra mile for you when it's needed.

3. Recognition and reward

Create adequate opportunity for team members to use their potential. Identify and utilise strengths. Whenever possible, allocate work and projects to make best use of these, and give some control and ownership, such as making people champions for specific areas.

Compensate for their areas of weakness by utilising the whole team. This gives them pride in what they do and they will appreciate that you've recognised where they do a good job, providing of course you're careful not to overburden or just dump these tasks on them.

Recognise and reward good performance, achievements and a job well-done. For many, that is all they need to feel encouraged. It always helps to know that their work is recognised. The easiest thing you can do is a genuine thank you.

A little something that's unexpected can evoke a very positive response. Give people the occasional treat. It doesn't have to cost the earth; just a token. But the thought it evokes will make a real difference.

For some people free time could be the most valuable gift you could give them. Allowing flexibility to go home early or come in late, to attend to a personal matter or just have a bit of fun can work wonders to their state of mind.

There are bound to be people in your team with a competitive spirit. So consider awards, competitions, or even a league table.

4. Communication

Look at the feedback from any employee engagement survey, exit interview or statistics on why projects fail and the one area that's invariably listed is poor (or a complete lack of) communication.

Your team not only want to feel included and involved, but they really do need to know what's going on to deliver a good job and look after your customers effectively.

Good communication impacts all three areas above.

Daily briefings are a good way to ensure everyone knows what's going on that could affect the operation or the customer experience in any way; no one wants to look uninformed or stupid especially in front of customers. What's happening where, what's available or not, who's not in today, what's on promotion, what's happening that customers may enquire about? ...Anything that affects that day's operation.

They also provide the perfect opportunity to gather feedback from them too on things which need addressing sooner rather than later.

Let your team know how the business is performing, and what this means to them. Communicate any changes happening in the business before they happen, and involve them in the process as much as possible. Whether the changes affect them directly or not, anything out of the norm will be unsettling and will have an impact on morale and subsequently productivity.

Use team meetings to ask your team for their feedback and show them you value their suggestions and ideas.

Never under estimate the impact of sitting down regularly with each member of the team on a one to one basis. These meetings should be scheduled so they can plan for them and around them. Nothing smacks more of "I'm not valued" than their one to one meetings being continually cancelled for the slightest reason.

Keep them simple so they are more likely to happen. Try focusing on these three core questions (or a version of these in your own words): *What's gone well? ~ What were you disappointed with? ~ What do you want to focus on next week/month/quarter?*

5. Development and growth

I often hear managers getting very frustrated that people in their team are not contributing as much as they'd like. They know, or at least suspect, they are capable of more, but for some reason some people are just not taking responsibility for making decisions or getting things done.

How do they see their role? If you (or maybe your predecessor) have always done the thinking for them, maybe that's accepted as the norm. Do they recognise that you'd like more from them, and if so what?

We so often think of development as grooming somebody for promotion. This might be one intention or outcome but even when we know that a team member has probably reached their peak, or we know full well they're not interested in progressing, that doesn't mean to say we let them stagnate.

A bored employee is unlikely to wow your customers!

Rather than making everybody mediocre at everything they do, tap into their strengths, talents and passions so they excel in certain areas, and work as a team to bridge the gaps in individuals' abilities or interests.

44

Give people exposure to other aspects of your business and an opportunity to experience different tasks which all leads to better understanding of your business as a whole and in turn creates confidence - for your team and your customers.

Money, money, money

Many assume money is a key motivator. There's no denying it's important; I'm sure none of us would work as hard as we do - if at all - if we weren't getting paid for it. But does it really motivate or engage people? Not long term. But taking it away will definitely leave people demotivated and disengaged.

So messing up their overtime, delaying their pay review, challenging legitimate expenses, or passing them over for promotion without being given a chance will all inevitably have a negative impact. In the same way as any other 'hygiene factors' such as safe working conditions, giving them the right tools and resources for the job, avoiding too much red tape.

No one is going to say "wow" when you provide them, but they'll certainly notice when they're missing.

Individual preferences

The golden rule is to treat others how you would wish to be treated. And that's certainly a good start. But the platinum rule is to treat others how **they** wish to be treated.

When I ask managers what's important to their team members it's usually quite revealing when I get an all too common responses of *"money and a quiet life"*, or *"I don't know"*.

The former might sometimes be the case to an extent, but sadly it's often an assumption. The only reason managers don't understand this is because they've never asked the question.

Spending time with team members and finding out what's important to them is just as important as you or your team spending time with customers, finding out their needs.

Ask what they enjoy about certain tasks and why; how they feel about particular aspects of their job. Conversely ask about the things that disappoint or frustrate them, and what they'd change if they could.

Whilst some love the sense of achievement or recognition others get a buzz from supporting others. Some love to have their say and see their ideas put into practice, whilst others are happiest when they're learning or being stretched.

Finding out about what people value outside work as well as in work can often be an insight. Ask casually about their weekend or what they have planned for the evening ahead or their day off, and show an interest in what they get up to in their spare time.

Talking about interests amongst the team can be useful for you, but can also elicit a sense of pride in the things they do outside work and helps each of your team understand what's important to their fellow team members.

So what?

But how does knowing what's important to someone outside work help you or them in work? Obviously it's not going to be possible to have them practicing their hobbies all day long!

But by looking at the attributes and skills for their activities when they're away from work can give us an inkling as to where their strengths lie and clues on how these can be applied in the workplace.

For example do they have a creative streak in them; do they get involved with highly competitive sports or activities; do they have a role of helping the community, supporting and caring.

Of course it won't always be practical or possible to fully incorporate their interests but if you aim to do this wherever you can you'll soon start to get the best from the team, which will invariably have a knock-on effect on customers too, notwithstanding making your life easier into the bargain!

So, stop trying to suss out what makes team members tick. Ask them!

Learn to let go

You can't be there 24/7. Trust your team to make decisions to do what's best. If they truly understand your customer service values and what's of most importance to a customer generally they'll work out the best solution.

A good leader should be prepared to muck in and roll their sleeves up when absolutely necessary; but this should be the exception rather than the rule.

If you find yourself getting frustrated that people are not doing things the way you want reflect on your training and explanations of your expectations. Give them feedback on how they're doing and compare it to their understanding of the standards.

When you've given the right training put your trust in them and let them get on with it. No one is going to feel comfortable having their boss looking over their shoulder the whole time.

If you give someone freedom and they misuse it they aren't right for your business. The right people will be happy to be empowered and will perform best with minimum supervision.

Expecting team members to seek your approval or get sign off every time is time wasting for you, demeaning for your team and at best frustrating for your customer.

People soon pick it up when you fail to trust or allocate any responsibility to them, leaving them doubting their own abilities.

Lack of confidence will prevent people getting on with things off their own bat. Encourage by assuring them that they have the skills and knowledge.

If you really are unsure of somebody's ability to deliver (even though they tell you they know what they're doing) get them to tell you or demonstrate to you how they would approach it. If you need to, make suggestions. Rather than instructing, reflect on what help and support they would need in order to achieve this and focus on that instead.

Keep their enthusiasm by asking for ideas and suggestions. Accept your way might not be the only way and they may have a better approach; one that saves time, gives a better result, or simply means they will feel more comfortable with it and are more likely to carry out the task.

If it's still not perfect set challenges to find a better way.

Actions speak louder than words

Everything you do in your business sends out a message. Not just to your customers, but to your team too.

We all know the importance of being a role model to your team. How you behave towards your customers and your team naturally sets the tone for how your team behave towards customers.

Treat your team with the same care, courtesy and respect as you'd like them to show to customers.

Your team only get confused if you're saying one thing but doing another. If they hear or see a hint of poor attitude to customers from supervisors or managers it sends the wrong message.

It's not just the obvious interaction with customers, but how you regard them in general. Bad mouthing or criticising a customer in their absence will certainly send the message that it's OK to be rude about customers, or even that customers are a nuisance or interruption to our job, rather than the very reason the job exists.

Acknowledge when you spot great examples of good practice. This helps reinforce to everyone what good service looks like. Recognise and reward those who go the extra mile and give exceptional customer service. Share successes and results so everyone recognises the impact.

Certain emotions or unresourceful states will inevitably have a knock-on impact on everyone around you –colleagues and customers alike. Being impatient, worried, angry, bored, frustrated, resistant, confused, irritated, flustered, tired or distracted all rub off.

We are all familiar with the mood Hoovers; you know... those who have a knack of sucking all that energy and enthusiasm from you like a Hoover.

When you, your team - any of us - are in these unresourceful states, if faced with challenges the tiniest problem can lead us to frustration or aggression; the slightest failure can lead to disappointment, blame or self-doubt; a hint of rejection can lead to anger or defensiveness.

Our physiology certainly influences our feelings and the feelings of people around us. So if we mooch around all day with shoulders dropped, hands in pockets, expressionless we're far more likely to elicit negative emotions, than if we're smiling, making eye contact and making gestures.

Smiling and laughing make us feel good and happy. And it's infectious... If you want your team to be enthusiastic, flexible, motivated, interested, confident, energetic, happy, welcoming, and friendly this has to **start with you**.

Actions

- On a scale of 1 to 10 how clear are your team on what's expected of them?

- How frequently do you sit down on a one-to-one basis with each member of your team?

- How well do you understand each of your team members individual preferences, strengths or motivations?

- How frequently do you get all your team together to talk about what's happening in your business and gather feedback from them on what could be improved?

- Who in your team deserves some recognition for a job well done? How will you reward this?

- Who in your team is ready to be stretched to avoid them becoming stale?

- What are you doing currently which one of your team could easily do as part of their development?

- On a scale of 1 to 10 how good a role model are you? And your senior team/line managers?

6

A Bad Workman Blames his Tools

A bad system will beat a good person
every time.

W. Edwards Deming

The saying goes *"a bad workman always blames his tools"*. But is it always the workmen who are at fault?

Unless you provide the right systems, resources and tools even the most talented and enthusiastic team members will struggle to deliver a consistent service.

Consistency

You're generally only as good as your customer's last experience. So get it wrong once and you need on average 10 positive experiences to outweigh the negative experience.

To build trust your customers should be getting the same level of service each and every time they buy from you so they won't be disappointed on their second, seventh or even 70th purchase.

To deliver the same consistent level of great customer service and customer experience you have to have systems in place, otherwise no two days will be the same and no two customer experiences will be the same.

Review your customer journey regularly to be sure to deliver on every occasion. With regular customers this means **continuous improvement,** as they will have set expectations, which you need to strive to **exceed on every visit.**

These don't need to be massive leaps; your aim should be for **Consistency +1%.** That way you'll always have something left for next time to impress those regulars!

Have systems for your team to follow to deliver this, whoever is on duty…. Not just your exceptional team members, even your average ones should be able to deliver outstanding service every day.

Equipment

The most obvious resource is the provision of the right equipment. This might be anything from reliable and up-to-date IT equipment, the appropriate tools of your trade (of the right quality and specification), through to the furniture, fixtures and fabric of your building. Equipment that is unreliable, slow or fails to do the job for which it was intended or having to cope with broken or poorly maintained tools can be a huge source of irritation for your team.

Consult with those who will be using the equipment before making investments.

Skimping on inferior quality equipment might help the initial cash flow, but in the end seldom pays off. However ask whether or not you need the all singing all dancing model, or just the basic. Why pay for extra features if they are seldom, if ever, needed?

Have a system in place for maintenance, whether this is done in house or with a contractor. Encourage team members to report problems promptly when the equipment doesn't appear to be functioning on all four cylinders, or gets damaged, rather than apportioning blame on them for causing the problem. Have a process which makes this quick and easy. Failure to report and deal with problems promptly not only leads to frustrations, and later accusations of whose fault it is, but could cost you dearly in the long run if it causes long-term damage.

Ensuring your team get the full training they need to get best use out of equipment is time well invested. Talk to your suppliers to support with this training. Ensure they understand the maintenance required and can spot quickly when there are faults that need reporting.

Remember too any equipment your customers will be using – any aspect of self-service will only cause frustration and disappointment for customers if it fails to deliver.

Products and consumables

You wouldn't expect a chef to produce a gourmet meal without the right ingredients. It would be very evident by the end result if the correct ingredients or the right quality have not been sourced.

So apply this same principle to the 'ingredients' of your business.

Whether it's the effectiveness of the cleaning products for your office cleaners, the quality of linen and toiletries for your hotel or the weight of the paper you use in your printing and packaging. It's easy for these to get overlooked. Each will have an impact on the finished result and how easy they are to use or work with, and whether they deliver what is required to the right standard.

Simple little things - even something as simple as the reliability of the pens you provide - can have an impact on the amount of effort needed from your team and on the quality of the end result, as well as the subconscious messages they send to your customers.

Time

Not having enough time to do the job to standard can be very sole destroying, particularly when people want to do a good job, but they just don't have the time to do that well. When people are under pressure inevitably they make mistakes, feel stressed and impact on your customers' experience.

Spend time with your team to identify how long a task should take. If it's taking longer than it should, assess what is causing the extra time. It might be down to the equipment, products or systems causing a bottleneck, or it may be down to lack of training on the best approach to complete the task.

If you give a team member additional responsibilities or duties, be realistic; unless you are increasing their hours something else will need to give to make way for this. Identify how that time can be made up. If you're not careful they could end up cutting corners on the most critical tasks rather than cutting out low priority ones.

Systems

A lack of systems means you and your team constantly have to reinvent the wheel and waste time which could otherwise be devoted to customers. Robust systems shouldn't mean robotic service. But by systemising the predictable and routine you leave time and scope to personalise your service by responding to individual customer needs.

The more customers are kept in mind for every decision taken in the business the easier it will be to give a consistent level of service to your customers. This includes the design of your internal as well as customer facing systems.

Check systems you have in place to enable your team to achieve the customer experience you expect. It can be incredibly demotivating for team members when they know what they should do but the system won't let them.

Having systems in place for when things go wrong is key if you want your team to take responsibility for putting things right without having to come running to you all the time e.g. dealing with customer complaints, wrong deliveries, faulty equipment.

Give people training in the systems. If they don't know what the system is, or, just as importantly understand why you have it, there's little chance they'll follow it.

Having minimum standard operating procedures provides a baseline so you can ensure everyone works by the same set of 'rules'; it only causes friction when someone sees someone else do something they are 'not allowed to do'. But, don't be so bound by red tape that people can't use their initiative and take control of situations when needed.

It's important to review your systems regularly. Are they achieving what they set out to do, or are they leading to doubling up or bottlenecks? Talk to the people who actually use the systems to check this, as often you may not be aware of any issues.

What needs a system?

Customer journey

Your customer journey map can be used as a framework through which customer experience is continuously measured and managed throughout the business.

Do a periodic walk through of your customer journey and conduct a self-audit against a checklist with measurable criteria for each stage. Schedule this into your routine, and continue to involve your team as they'll pick up on things you become blinkered to.

Direct customer feedback

Whether it's asking customers directly for their feedback at the point of purchase or whether it's as a follow up make sure it happens on a routine basis and there is a system in place for:

- Asking - when to ask, what format, how often, what questions

- Capturing - what gets recorded, how, where and when

- Acting on it - how this gets reviewed, who takes responsibility

- Following up with customers - how, who and when

Customer behaviour and reaction

Be observant and spot problems before it's too late. A regular order that's less than normal, a frequent customer who hasn't visited for a while, clients not returning your calls, a change in tone from a customer, picking up on non-verbal cues or a throw away comment that the customer isn't completely happy, increased complaints on a particular product or service.

Build this into your team briefings so you have a way of picking up on these warning signs before they become an issue.

Accept that whatever people have to say about your business some of that will find its way onto social media. But with so many social media platforms potentially talking about you how do you keep tabs? As a minimum set up Google Alerts for your name and business so you know when you're being talked about. Although you won't get instant feedback you can set this up so you get notifications as they happen, daily or weekly. If you wait a week to find out it's invariably too late!

Test and measure

If you're tracking your numbers you'll soon know when things are not right. It won't necessarily tell you why, but at least it should set the alarms bells ringing so you can investigate. Putting it down to "the market is slow at the moment" or "the competition" won't rectify the problem. Make service your key point of differentiation and find a way to wow your customers so they stay naturally loyal to YOU, and keep coming back whatever the market or the competition is up to.

Complaints procedures

With the best will in the world there are things that go wrong; accidents happen, things get missed or events occur that are totally out of your control. So establish a protocol to deal with these which enable your team to lessen the impact on your customers' experience and limit the potential damage to your reputation.

Team Communication

Keep them in the loop so they are kept up to date. Product knowledge is a must.

We've already discussed the importance of briefings so your team knows what's happening on a day-to-day basis, so ensure these are scheduled and part of your routine, not a one off exercise.

Customer Communication

You'll no doubt have something in place for customers from a marketing perspective. Customers always appreciate being informed of anything that's exclusive to them, which makes them feel particularly special or cared for.

But there are times when you need to communicate with them from a service perspective, by way of pre-empting or avoiding a service dip.

Customers are far more understanding of the situation if they're kept informed or forewarned of potential problems. For example, if you know that you're likely to be busy at certain times of the day, make every effort to let your customers know this. If you let them know when the quieter times are, this not only helps them, it could even out the peaks and troughs for you too.

When you know something is unavailable; maybe something that is a popular feature or product that is not available for whatever reason, give people as much notice as possible either through your website, when ordering or booking if relevant, prior to travel or on arrival to minimise disappointment.

So have a system in place so your team can be proactive in your customer communications.

People

Put processes in place that will help you flag up when you might need extra manpower, when resources are going to be stretched, so you can act on it beforehand.

What happens when a team member leaves, or goes on holiday? What impact does that have on the rest of the team? The effects may be felt in other departments too, if they are dependent on this person for information or ordering, for example.

Are there skills shortages in certain areas, which only affect you once in a while (e.g. certain types of events, or when people are on holiday) but when they do, they put pressure on the whole team and impact customers?

The more flexibility you have in your team the better. This does not mean you make everyone a Jack of all trades, but ensure there is always more than just one person who is able to perform each task, so there is an element of cover, and the whole place does not fall apart, just because one person is off sick.

This applies to third party providers too. What happens if they are short staffed? What back up do they have to ensure your customers' experience does not suffer? Spell out your expectations, and put a process in place so you can be made aware if there are any potential shortfalls before they impact your customers.

Recruitment

The majority of businesses wait until they have a vacancy before they think about recruitment. This inevitably puts a strain on the existing team and ultimately affects service.

Instead of being reactive, create a system which allows you to have on hand a pool of potential people who are waiting in the wings to come and join your business, and can hit the ground running as quickly as possible.

Build customer service standards and training into induction, so no one has the chance to get into bad habits. Setting expectations from day one helps everyone maintain consistency. Allocate responsibility for induction and draw up a standard induction programme which is available to all managers for their new starters.

Even if you recruit someone with extensive experience in customer service, train them from scratch in **your** way of doing things so they fully understand **your service culture**.

Actions

- In your next team meeting review your customer service journey and discuss how the service journey is impacted by:

  - equipment
  - systems
  - time constraints
  - where people are stretched
  - where it's dependent on one key person

- Create an action plan to address potential problem or risk areas

- Review your customer feedback process:
  What feedback have you had recently that:

  - flags up issues?
  - identifies potential opportunities?

7

A stick of rock

Culture drives great results.

Jack Welch

If you make customer service part of the day-to-day focus, it soon becomes second nature for people to help and support one another in delivering outstanding service.

Service is more than a department.

It's everyone's responsibility.

Your service ethos should be part your DNA and reflected in everything you do. Like a stick of rock – no matter where you break it the core message is still the same.

This means it's more than just enthusing your customer facing teams about the value of every customer, because it isn't just the responsibility of the sales team, the receptionists or customer service desk.

Everyone in your business contributes in some way to the customer experience either directly or indirectly (or why are they there?). This includes how your support teams not only interact and serve your external customers, but how they serve the **internal customer.** How your customer facing teams are supported and treated internally will inevitably have a **knock on effect on your customers.**

Your entire team must understand the basics: what good service looks like and recognise the role they play in creating the customer experience. Not by having endless policies, but by having the freedom to use their initiative to do **what's right for the customer;** be they internal or external.

Your **customer service ethos** has to be demonstrated by **everyone** in your business not just the front line team.

Create a Culture of Putting Customers First

How highly you value customers is also communicated through your systems and practices. To what extent are you prepared to put yourself out for the benefit of a customer?

This isn't just obvious things such as being available for your customers when it's convenient for them rather than you. (One of my pet hates is businesses - particularly customer service desks - that only open Monday to Friday 9 till 5 yet they support customers who invariably only have time or access during non-working hours.)

What message does it send when the powers that be clearly see themselves as being far more important than the customer? If you play golf I'm sure you'll know what I mean when you see all the plum parking spaces immediately outside the clubhouse being reserved for the committee. Or in corporate offices where there are 3 or 4 empty parking spaces immediately outside the front door reserved for the chief executive and his/her entourage, while visitors have to park way down the car park (if they can find a parking space at all that is!). Just what sort of message does that convey to a customer, and in turn what message does that convey to your team about the importance you place on customers?

It goes far beyond just parking spaces. Simple things such as interrupting a member of staff who is talking to a customer without so much as acknowledging the customer; not trusting team members by delegating authority to do what they think is best for the customer; blaming the customer or quibbling over minor customer disputes. All these send the message we put ourselves before the customer.

What gets measured gets done

If you're stressing the importance of the customer experience and to keep the customer happy, but all your metrics are centred on the bottom line and profitability this will not put the focus on customers! Put as much time and effort into monitoring your customer service as you do your profitability.

Continuous improvement

Create a culture of continuous improvement. Challenge your team members to come forward with suggestions on how things can be improved, not just for the customer but to make their lives easier too. Shaving 5 minutes off a task in one area can free up 5 more minutes to spend caring for customers elsewhere.

Getting feedback from both your customers and your team is key to making continuous improvements in your service.

But team members are often very reluctant to ask for feedback for fear they're going to hear something they don't want to, or have to deal with something they don't know how to.

It's all too easy for them to ask customers to feedback to a manager, fill out a comment's slip or respond to something online.

So it's important they recognise the need for first-hand feedback there and then.

And then have a system in place to collate this, and most importantly ACT ON IT.

Positive feedback can be a really big boost for the team. Ensure this gets shared, and the quicker you share it amongst those who have contributed to the feedback the more impact it will have. Even for those not involved or contributing to that customer's comments it helps illustrate the impact of good service and a great customer experience, so use it to reinforce good practice.

Be a good employer

Recruit only those who fit your service culture, rather than focusing purely on skills.

All too often businesses recruit on aptitude, but fire on attitude. Unless they have the right attitude, values and beliefs to fit your culture you have little chance of changing it. So recruit first on attitude then on aptitude.

We've effectively already defined your customer avatar. Why not do the same for your team? What are the values, beliefs and attitudes that a person needs to demonstrate to fit in with the culture of your business and really excel in that role.

Create a culture where positive attitudes prevail, and build a reputation as a good employer so you attract the best people. If your business is somewhere people love to work, they'll happily become advocates and ambassadors for your business. That way when you come to recruit you'll be able to do so wisely and more likely have a steady stream of people queueing up!

A prerequisite is looking after your existing team; they are far more likely to recommend you to others and spread the word it's a great place to work. Monitor the reputation of your business; listen to what your staff say, especially those who leave.

The power to do what's best

If you make customer service part of the day-to-day focus rather than a periodic training exercise it will become second nature for people to help and support one another in putting the customer first.

By creating an environment where it's okay to ask questions, to admit you don't know all the answers, and to put forward suggestions to improve your customers' experience gives your team the confidence to think for themselves and take whatever action is going to give the customer the best outcome.

Create a culture where your team have permission to do something spontaneous if they see an opportunity to enhance the customers' experience.

Actions

- On a scale of 1 to 10 how well do your support teams serve the internal customers?

- What habits or practices are there in your business which could suggest to a customer they're not your number one priority?

- What metrics do you have in place for monitoring your customer service/customer experience?

- What systems or processes do you have in place to spot opportunities for continuous improvement?

- What criteria do you use to attract/recruit team members with the right attitude, values and beliefs to fit in with your customer service culture?

- How much freedom do your team have to do something spontaneous if they see an opportunity to enhance your customers experience?

- Reflecting on your responses to the above questions what are your priority actions?

8

In summary

> Success is nothing more than a few simple disciplines, practiced every day.
>
> Jim Rohn

When it comes to the overall customer experience your team can be your point of differentiation. A happy, involved and confident team can work wonders on your customers and their perception of the service they receive.

What to do next

Now it's time to translate these principles into your world. Here are 11 questions to get you started.

1. What is your number one goal for your customer experience and engaging your team in customer service improvement?

2. How will you know when you have achieved it?

3. Where are you now?

4. What have you already implemented towards your goal?

5. What training, support and resources does your team need to help them achieve this?

6. If you could start one thing tomorrow, what would it be?

7. If anything were to stand in your way, what would it be?

8. What could you do to overcome this?

9. Who could help you?

10. If you had a mentor or coach to help with this, who would you chose?

11. What action could you take in the next 24 hours towards your goal?

Download your bonus Superstar Resources, including tips, tools and templates at www.creatingservicesuperstars.com.

About the Author

Caroline Cooper has over **25 years' experience** in helping businesses develop their managers enabling them to get the best from their teams to create a **loyal team** who create **loyal customers.**

She founded Naturally Loyal on 3 strong beliefs:

- The happier your team the happier your customers.

- Customer service training is just the tip of the iceberg when it comes to delivering a great customer experience. It requires a whole infrastructure to support it.

- The more a business can develop their teams in house the greater the ownership and more sustainable it will be.

Her mission is to teach others so they can find their talents and strengths so they become as self-sufficient as possible to give flexibility (and make training budgets go a whole lot further!)

She works with businesses in 4 ways:

- Working one-on-one focusing on **developing leadership skills.**

- Writing **bespoke training material** to be delivered by the in-house team.

- Providing **affordable online resources** through her membership site.

- Providing tools and guidance to measure and improve **employee engagement.**

If you'd like more information on her services please email: service@naturallyloyal.com

Lightning Source UK Ltd.
Milton Keynes UK
UKOW06f0808050117

291430UK00001B/57/P